VOTE
VOTE
VOTE
AF604604

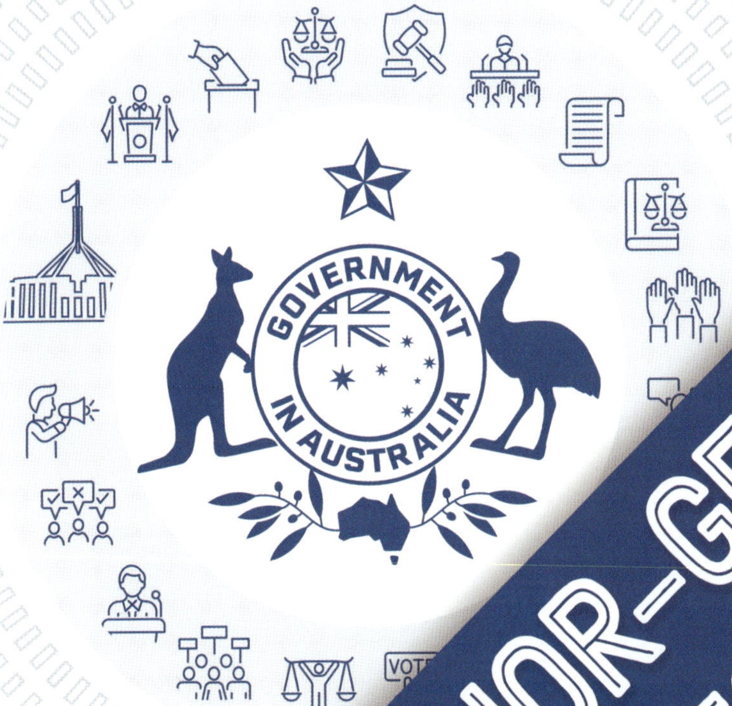

GOVERNOR-GENERAL OR PRESIDENT?

John Lesley

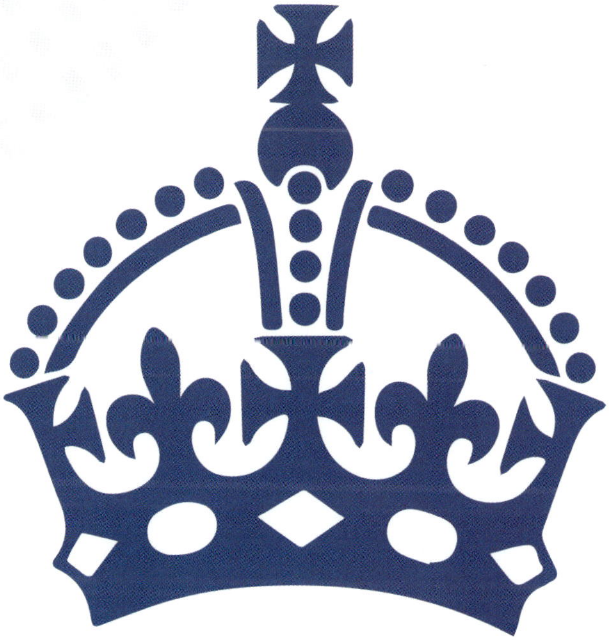

First Published 2025 by
Redback Publishing
Suite 6, 13a Narabang Way,
Belrose NSW 2085
Australia

www.redbackpublishing.com
orders@redbackpublishing.com

ISBN 978-1-761401-12-1

Author: John Lesley
Editor: Caroline Thomas
Designer: Redback Publishing

Original illustrations © Redback Publishing 2025
Originated by Redback Publishing

A catalogue record for this book is available from the National Library of Australia

CONTENTS

AUSTRALIA'S GOVERNOR-GENERAL

The Monarch's Representative

Australia has a Governor-General as a result of having inherited a British, Westminster System of government. In this system, the Monarch of the United Kingdom is the Head of State. In Australia, since the Monarch is not present, the Governor-General acts in their place.

Ceremonial Duties

The Governor-General's role includes ceremonial duties, just as we have seen the Monarch performing in Britain, such as giving awards to people who have made outstanding contributions to the nation.

Medals of the Order of Australia are often presented to recipients by the Governor-General

Parliament House, Canberra

Parliamentary Role

In Parliament, the Governor-General has the important role of approving Bills passed by the Parliament, and thus making them laws that all people in Australia have to obey.

WHO CHOOSES THE GOVERNOR-GENERAL?

Constitutional Rules

The Australian Constitution describes how the Governor-General is to be appointed as follows:

"A Governor-General appointed by the Queen shall be Her Majesty's representative in the Commonwealth, and shall have and may exercise in the Commonwealth during the Queen's pleasure, but subject to this Constitution, such powers and functions of the Queen as Her Majesty may be pleased to assign to him."

The Constitution came into force in 1901, so the Monarch mentioned above is Queen Victoria. This wording also applies to the current Monarch, King Charles III.

Commonwealth of Australia Constitution Act.

AN ACT

TO

Constitute the Commonwealth of Australia.

Cap. 12

[9th July 1900]

Queen Victoria

Advice to the Monarch

In practice, the Monarch acts on the advice of the Prime Minister of Australia when appointing a new Governor-General.

King Charles III

The Coat of Arms of Australia

Serving Society

The person appointed as Governor-General is usually someone who has had a long career in service to society, such as through being elected to Parliament, serving in the Australian Defence Force, or having held academic positions.

ROLE IN PARLIAMENT

Separation of Powers

The Separation of Powers of government into three independent sections is a basic principle of a Westminster System of government. The Australian Governor-General has a role to play in all three of these sections. The three sections of the Federal Australian Government are:

The Parliament

includes the House of Representatives, the Senate and the Governor-General. In Parliament, the Governor-General is responsible for signing Bills into laws.

The Executive

Includes the Prime Minister, Ministers and the Governor-General. In the Federal Executive Council, the Governor-General heads meetings that discuss legislation.

The Judicature

includes the High Court of Australia and the Federal courts. In the Judiciary, the Governor-General appoints High Court judges after being advised on suitable candidates by the Prime Minister.

The Upper House of the Australian Parliament

Bills and Laws

Even though a Bill might be passed by both Houses of the Australian Parliament, it does not become a law until it is signed by the Governor-General. In theory, the Governor-General has enormous power to overturn the will of the people, as expressed through their elected representatives, by not signing a Bill. In practice, this power has never been put into action, although Bills have occasionally been returned to the Houses of Parliament for changes to be made.

The House of Representatives

Opening and Dissolving Parliament

When a Federal election is called by the Prime Minister, which is at least once every three years, the Governor-General then dissolves Parliament. As a result, all the Members of the House of Representatives lose their positions. If they want to return to Parliament, they need to go back to the people and seek to be elected again.

Half the number of Senators also lose their positions and need to seek re-election to return to the Senate.

After a Federal election, the Governor-General invites the leader of the winning party, or coalition of parties, to form Government. The Governor-General stands in for the Monarch at the opening of Parliament. They also swear in new Ministers and the new Prime Minister of the Government.

Limited Attendance

When a new Parliament sits for the first time after an election, the Governor-General opens the session with a speech made in the Senate. This is the only time a Governor-General is present at a sitting of Parliament.

Appointing and Dismissing

The Governor-General appoints High Court judges, the Prime Minister, Ministers and the Chief of the Australian Defence Force. The Governor-General also has the power to dismiss Ministers. In practice, all of these powers are normally performed on the advice of the Prime Minister.

Oaths or Affirmations of Office

The Governor-General officially swears-in judges of the High Court and Federal courts, as well as Government Ministers, including the Prime Minister, by requiring them to take the Oath or Affirmation of Office. The Oath includes a plea to God, but the Affirmation does not.

Oath

I, A.B., do swear that I will be faithful and bear true allegiance to Her Majesty Queen Victoria, Her heirs and successors according to law. SO HELP ME GOD!

Affirmation

I, A.B., do solemnly and sincerely affirm and declare that I will be faithful and bear true allegiance to Her Majesty Queen Victoria, Her heirs and successors according to law.

The name of the reigning Monarch is used in place of the reference to Queen Victoria.

RESERVE POWERS

British Traditions

The Governor-General has some powers that are not included in the Australian Constitution. These are called 'reserve powers', and they are based on British traditions in which the Monarch has certain powers over aspects of the operation of Parliament.

Special and Unusual Circumstances

The reserve powers of the Governor-General in Australia only apply in very special and unusual circumstances. They include the power to remove or appoint a Prime Minister in the middle of a term of Parliament.

Historical Controversies

The use of the reserve powers on four occasions in the past caused controversy amongst the general public.

Lord Northcote

1904

Governor-General Lord Northcote refused to dissolve the House of Representatives to allow for a federal election.

1905

Governor-General Lord Northcote allowed Alfred Deakin to replace George Reid as Prime Minister without an election.

Alfred Deakin

William Humble Ward

1909

Governor-General William Humble Ward allowed an unelected coalition of parties to form government.

1975

Governor-General Sir John Kerr sacked Prime Minister Gough Whitlam, forcing a federal election.

Sir John Kerr

MEETING & GREETING

Public Duties

The public duties that we have seen the British Monarch performing in the United Kingdom are carried out by the Governor-General in Australia. These include making visits to communities in distress, meeting with visiting dignitaries as well as ordinary people, and giving awards and other encouragement to people who have made outstanding contributions to Australia.

In performing these duties, the Governor-General represents not only the Monarch but also the whole of the Australian people, without regard to any party political divisions.

Congratulatory Messages

Acting on behalf of the Monarch, the Governor-General sends congratulatory messages to Australians celebrating significant birthdays and wedding anniversaries. This is not automatic, and a request has to be made, along with supporting documentation of the event being celebrated.

Heads of State

There are different official welcoming ceremonies for the leaders of other nations, depending on whether the person is a Head of State (such as a King), or a Head of Government (such as a visiting Prime Minister).

Heads of State are welcomed by the Governor-General at a ceremony that includes a military guard of honour and a twenty-one-gun salute.

Heads of Government are welcomed at a ceremony hosted by the Prime Minister.

Military guard of honour

REPUBLIC?

A republic, such as the USA, does not have a king or queen as its Head of State. In the USA, a President assumes this role.

In contrast, Australia's form of government is both a constitutional monarchy and a representative democracy. The Governor-General represents the Monarch in Australia and therefore acts on their behalf as the local Head of State.

What Would an Australian Republic Look Like?

If Australia were a republic and had a President as its Head of State, this could result in having a government that was similar to the one in the USA, or the new government structure could be restyled in a particular Australian way.

For example, Australia could decide to keep the title Governor-General for the Head of State, rather than use the term President.

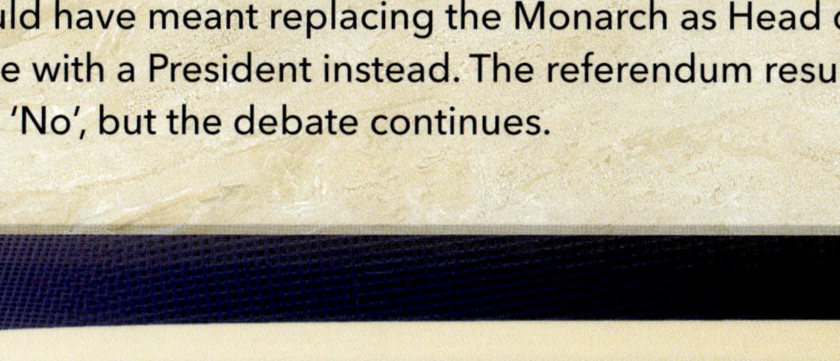

Republic Referendum

There was a referendum in 1999 in which Australian citizens were asked to decide if they wanted to change the Constitution and become a republic. This would have meant replacing the Monarch as Head of State with a President instead. The referendum result was 'No', but the debate continues.

Many of the roles of the existing Governor-General might remain similar. The major difference would be that there would be no allegiance to a Monarch.

The branches of the Australian Defence Force would no longer begin with the title 'Royal', as in Royal Australian Navy (RAN), and Royal Australian Air Force (RAAF).

STATE GOVERNORS

Each of the six Australian States has its own State Governor. State Governors perform similar roles to those of the Governor-General but at the State Parliament level.

Like the Governor-General, State Governors are appointed by and represent the Monarch, on the advice of the State Premiers. In the Northern Territory and Norfolk Island, an Administrator represents the Governor-General.

Darwin

Western Australia

Perth

King Charles III

The Government Houses in each state pictured on this map are the official residences of their respective State Premiers/Administrator.

Independent Representation

All the State Governors are independent of Australia's Governor-General. They represent the Monarch for their own State, without any need to consult the Governor-General.

Queensland's House Rule

Queensland's Government is unicameral, which means it only has one House of Parliament. This is the Legislative Assembly or Lower House.

Queensland abolished its Upper House, the Legislative Council, in 1922, but still keeps the room in perfect condition. The room is used by the State Governor when giving their speech during the opening of a new Parliament. This follows the tradition of both the British and Australian Parliaments, since the Monarch or Governor never enter the Lower House.

COMMANDER-IN-CHIEF

An Anzac Day memorial service

21-gun salute at the Parliament House forecourt

The Commander-in-Chief of the Australian Defence Force is the Governor-General.

The Governor-General attends military parades and special occasions such as Anzac Day. They also appoint senior military officers who handle the administration and operation of the Defence Forces.

GOVERNMENT HOUSE

The Governor-General has two official residences:

- **Yarralumla, Government House in Canberra**
- **Admiralty House in Sydney**

Yarralumla, Government House in Canberra

Government House at Yarralumla is the official residence of the Governor-General in Canberra. It is also the main administrative centre for the Office. The large property is listed on the Commonwealth Heritage list and was once farmland. The Australian Government bought the house and land in 1913 and in 1925 began renovating the house for use as the Governor-General's official residence.

Admiralty House in Sydney

The Governor General's Sydney residence is located in the suburb of Kirribilli. In 1913, Admiralty House was used by the Australian Government as a residence for the Governor-General. The residence was closed during the Depression and reopened in 1936. It became an official property of the Australian Government in 1948, on condition that it only be used as a residence for the Governor-General.

G.G. FAST FACTS

The Governor-General has no definite length of time in the position but usually carries out duties for five years.

The Governor-General represents the Monarch as the Head of State.

The person appointed as the Governor-General also becomes Commander-in-Chief of the Australian Defence Force, which includes the Army, Navy and Air Force.

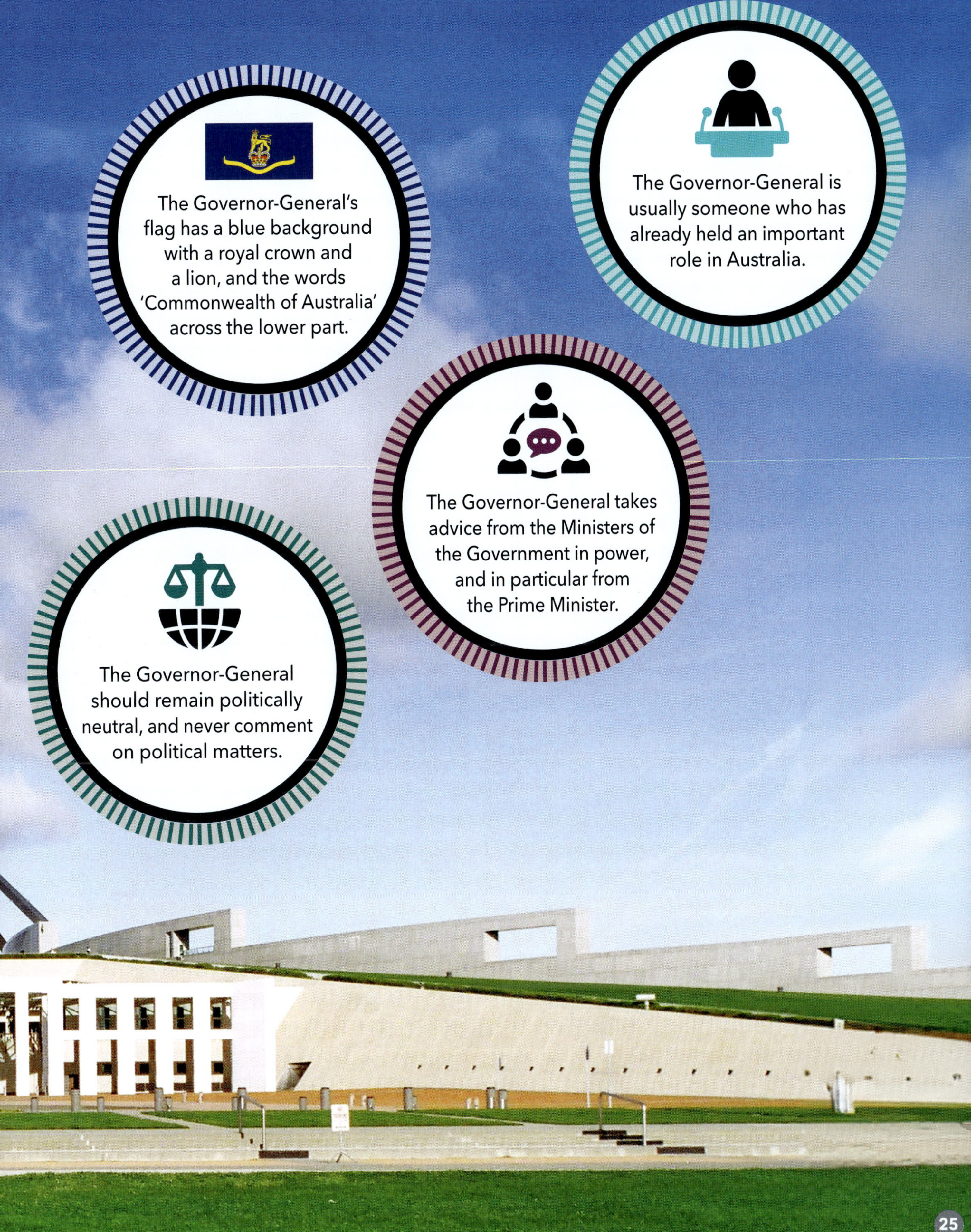
The Governor-General's flag has a blue background with a royal crown and a lion, and the words 'Commonwealth of Australia' across the lower part.
The Governor-General is usually someone who has already held an important role in Australia.
The Governor-General takes advice from the Ministers of the Government in power, and in particular from the Prime Minister.
The Governor-General should remain politically neutral, and never comment on political matters.

GOVERNORS-GENERAL

Since Federation in 1901, and until 2024, there have been 28 Governors-General of the Commonwealth of Australia.

In Office: 1965-1969
16
Richard Casey

In Office: 1961-1965
15
William De L'Isle

In Office: 1960-1961
14
William Morrison

In Office: 1953-1960
13
William Slim

In Office: 1947-1953
12
William McKell

In Office: 1945-1947
11
Prince Henry, Duke of Gloucester

In Office: 1936-1945
10
Alexander Hore-Ruthven

In Office: 1931-1936
9
Isaac Isaacs

In Office: 1925-1931
8
John Baird

In Office: 1920-1925
7
Henry Forster

In Office: 1914-1920
6
Ronald Munro-Ferguson

In Office: 1911-1914
5
Thomas Denman

In Office: 1908-1911
4
William Ward

In Office: 1904-1908
3
Henry Northcote

In Office: 1903-1904
2
Hallam Tennyson

In Office: 1901-1903
1
John Hope

ORDER OF AUSTRALIA

Queen Elizabeth II

Service and Achievement

The Order of Australia is a prestigious award system which honours people for their outstanding service or exceptional achievement. The Order of Australia awards are administered by the Office of the Governor-General, and they date from 1975 during the reign of Queen Elizabeth II.

Structure and Distinction

The Monarch is the Head of the Order, and the Governor-General is the Chancellor of the Order.

The Order of Australia is separate from Australian of the Year, which is a system of honours supported by the Department of the Prime Minister and Cabinet.

Former Governor-General Quentin Bryce invests Major General Tim McOwan AO DSC CSM with the insignia of Officer of the Order of Australia

Medal of the Order of Australia

Four Levels

The Order of Australia has four levels, plus a Military Division.

Companion of the Order of Australia (AC)

Officer of the Order of Australia (AO)

Member of the Order of Australia (AM)

Medal of the Order of Australia (OAM)

Australia Day celebrations on Sydney Harbour

Dates and Ceremonies

The awards are announced twice each year, on Australia Day (26 January) and on The King's Birthday (second Monday in June).

The award recipients attend a ceremony that may be presided over by either the Governor-General or the State Governor or Territory Administrator of the region in which the recipient lives.

WHAT ABOUT 1788?

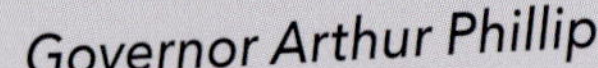
Governor Arthur Phillip

Question

Does Australia's Governor-General hold the same position as Governor Arthur Phillip did when he founded the first British colony in New South Wales back in 1788?

Answer

No!

The person who can trace their official role back to that of Arthur Phillip in 1788 is the Governor of the State of New South Wales.

The role of Governor-General had never existed before 1901, when the Commonwealth of Australia was created.

The first Governor-General of Australia was John Hope (Lord Hopetoun) in 1901, not Arthur Phillip in 1788.

John Hope (Lord Hopetoun)

GLOSSARY

ceremonial referring to the rules for a special event

congratulatory referring to good wishes based on a success

controversy debate over whether something is right or proper

dignitaries important people

guard of honour rows of military personnel or civilians who stand and welcome someone

monarch king or queen

plea request

prestigious very important and respected

principle basis for a system of belief

recipient person who receives something

term length of time for a Parliament

tradition way in which things used to be done

INDEX

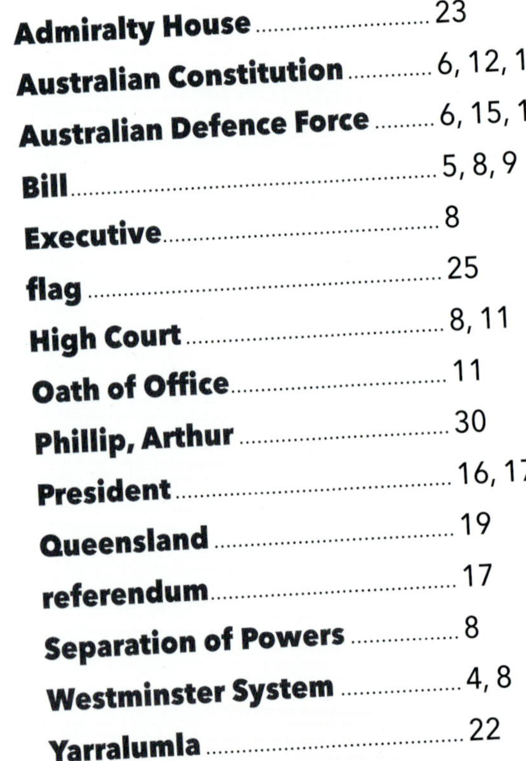

Acknowledgements
Abbreviations: l–left, r–right, b–bottom, t–top, c–centre, m–middle

We would like to thank the following for permission to reproduce photographs (images © Shutterstock unless otherwise stated): p2tl John, CC BY-SA 2.0 <https://creativecommons.org/licenses/by-sa/2.0>, via Wikimedia Commons, p2tr Drop of Light/Shutterstock.com, p3bl EQRoy/Shutterstock.com, p4tr Tralis2, CC BY-SA 4.0 <https://creativecommons.org/licenses/by-sa/4.0>, via Wikimedia Commons, p6ml National Archives of Australia, Public domain, via Wikimedia Commons, p6bl Bertha Müller, Public domain, via Wikimedia Commons, p7tr Muhammad Aamir Sumsum/Shutterstock.com, p8tl FiledIMAGE/Shutterstock.com, P8bl Greg Brave/Shutterstock.com, p9tc EQRoy/Shutterstock.com, p10tl FiledIMAGE/Shutterstock.com, p13bml Unidentified photographer, CC BY-SA 4.0 <https://creativecommons.org/licenses/by-sa/4.0>, via Wikimedia Commons, p15bl Drop of Light/Shutterstock.com, p17tl Nils Versemann/Shutterstock.com, p18bl Tennessee Witney/Shutterstock.com, p18tr Elly in the Top End/Shutterstock.com, p18br munhotobank.com.au/Shutterstock.com, p19bl Alex Cimbal/Shutterstock.com, p19ml Kgbo, CC BY-SA 4.0 <https://creativecommons.org/licenses/by-sa/4.0>, via Wikimedia Commons, p19m Aleksandar Todorovic/Shutterstock.com, p19br Barrylb, Public domain, via Wikimedia Commons, p18-19c Drop of Light/Shutterstock.com, p19t Wirestock Creators/Shutterstock.com, p19b GTS Productions/Shutterstock.com, p21t IOIO IMAGES/Shutterstock.com, p22 John, CC BY-SA 2.0 <https://creativecommons.org/licenses/by-sa/2.0>, via Wikimedia Commons, p23tc FiledIMAGE/Shutterstock.com, p23bl cvotography/Shutterstock.com, p24mc doublelee/Shutterstock.com, p25br PUIREN M RAMOS/Shutterstock.com, p26 Sam Mostyn: attribute gg.gov.au, Zelman Cowen, National Archives of Australia - Creative Commons Attribution 3.0 Australia Licence, CC BY 3.0 <https://creativecommons.org/licenses/by/3.0>, via Wikimedia Commons, Sir Ninian Stephen, Office of the Official Secretary to the Governor-General, on behalf of the Commonwealth of Australia, CC BY 3.0 <https://creativecommons.org/licenses/by/3.0>, via Wikimedia Commons, William Deane, Australian Paralympic Committee, CC BY-SA 3.0 <https://creativecommons.org/licenses/by-sa/3.0>, via Wikimedia Commons, Dr Peter Hollingworth, Governor-General of Australia, CC BY 3.0 <https://creativecommons.org/licenses/by/3.0>, via Wikimedia Commons, Michael Jeffery, Governor-General of Australia, CC BY 3.0 <https://creativecommons.org/licenses/by/3.0>, via Wikimedia Commons, Quentin Bryce, gg.gov.au, via Wikimedia Commons, David Hurley, Office of the Governor-General of Australia, CC BY 3.0 <https://creativecommons.org/licenses/by/3.0>, via Wikimedia Commons, p28tl State of Queensland, CC BY 4.0 <https://creativecommons.org/licenses/by/4.0>, via Wikimedia Commons, p28bc ButterStick, Public domain, via Wikimedia Commons, p29tl Tralis2, CC BY-SA 4.0 <https://creativecommons.org/licenses/by-sa/4.0>, via Wikimedia Commons, p29tl Tralis2, CC BY-SA 4.0 <https://creativecommons.org/licenses/by-sa/4.0>, via Wikimedia Commons, p29mr aiyoshi597/Shutterstock.com, p32tl, br FiledIMAGE/Shutterstock.com, p32bl Tralis2, CC BY-SA 4.0 <https://creativecommons.org/licenses/by-sa/4.0>, via Wikimedia Commons

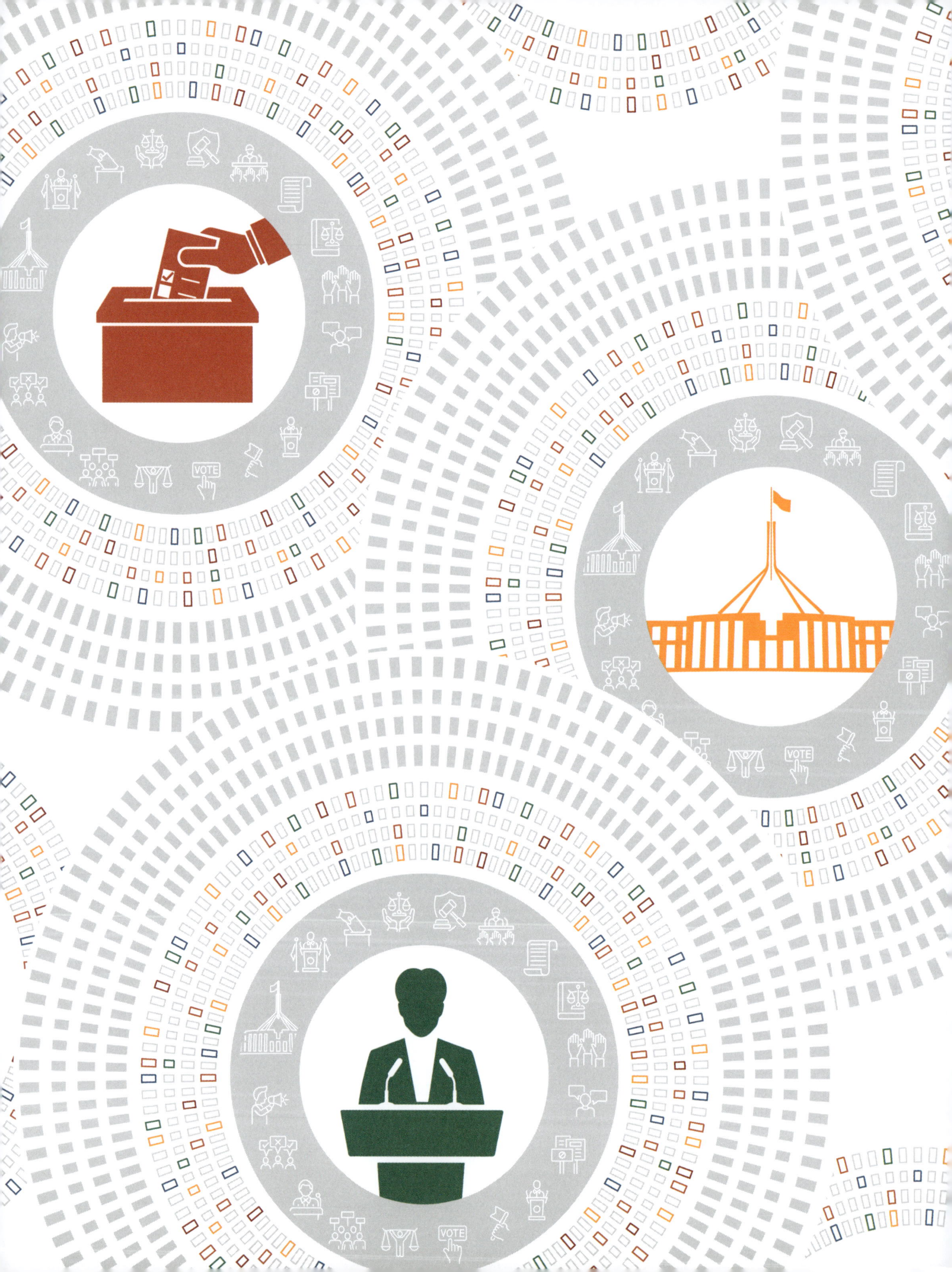
VOTE
VOTE
VOTE